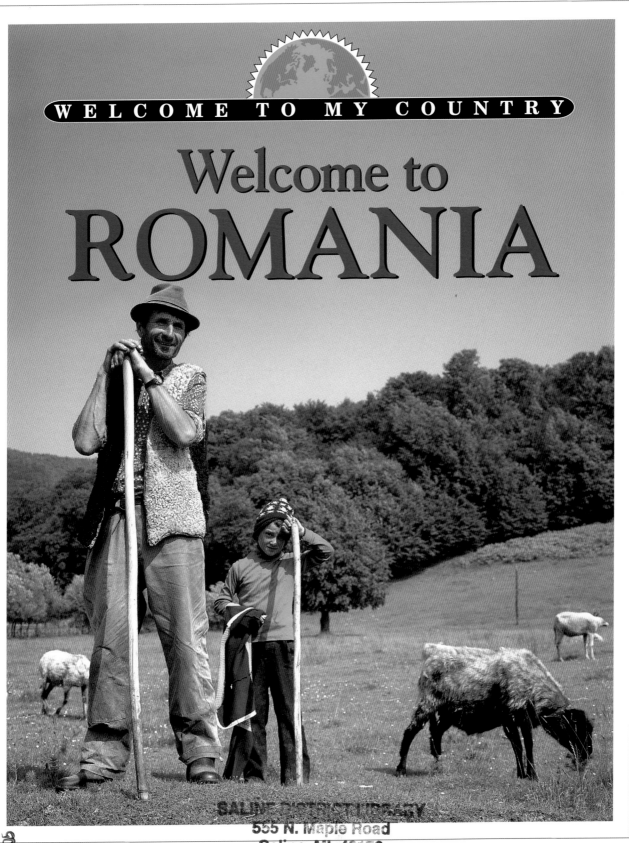

WELCOME TO MY COUNTRY

Welcome to
ROMANIA

Gareth Stevens Publishing
A WORLD ALMANAC EDUCATION GROUP COMPANY

Written by
GRACE PUNDYK

Edited by
MELVIN NEO

Edited in USA by
JENETTE DONOVAN GUNTLY

Designed by
GEOSLYN LIM

Picture research by
SUSAN JANE MANUEL

First published in North America in 2005 by
Gareth Stevens Publishing
A World Almanac Education Group Company
330 West Olive Street, Suite 100
Milwaukee, Wisconsin 53212 USA

Please visit our web site at
www.garethstevens.com
For a free color catalog describing
Gareth Stevens Publishing's list of high-quality
books and multimedia programs,
call 1-800-542-2595 (USA) or
1-800-387-3178 (Canada).
Gareth Stevens Publishing's fax: (414) 332-3567.

© **MARSHALL CAVENDISH INTERNATIONAL (ASIA)
PRIVATE LIMITED 2004**
Originated and designed by
Times Editions Marshall Cavendish
An imprint of Marshall Cavendish International (Asia) Pte Ltd
A member of Times Publishing Limited
Times Centre, 1 New Industrial Road
Singapore 536196
http://www.timesone.com.sg/te

Library of Congress Cataloging-in-Publication Data
Pundyk, Grace.
Welcome to Romania / by Grace Pundyk.
p. cm. — (Welcome to my country)
Includes bibliographical references and index.
ISBN 0-8368-2567-5 (lib. bdg.)
1. Romania — Juvenile literature. I. Title. II. Series.
DR205.P86   2004
949.8—dc22   2004045332

Printed in Singapore

1 2 3 4 5 6 7 8 9 08 07 06 05 04

Contents

Words that appear in the glossary are printed in **boldface** type the first time they occur in the text.

Welcome to Romania!

Romania is located in southeastern Europe. The country is a beautiful land of rivers, lakes, mountains, and plains. Romania is rich in cultural traditions, which Romanians have fought to keep during centuries of war and **invasions**. Let's explore stunning Romania and learn about its interesting people!

Opposite: At the end of this street in Bucharest sits the huge Palace of Parliament. It is one of the world's largest buildings.

Below: Many men and women in Romania work on farms. Farming is one of the country's largest industries.

The Flag of Romania

Romania's flag is divided into three sections of blue, yellow, and red. While the origin of the flag's colors is uncertain, some believe they were part of flags raised during battles against the invading Ottoman Turks and Hungarians.

The Land

Romania's land area is 91,675 square miles (237,500 square kilometers). It is surrounded by five countries, which include Hungary, Ukraine, Moldova, Serbia and Montenegro, and Bulgaria. To the east, the Black Sea creates about 140 miles (225 kilometers) of coastline. The Black Sea coast, which lies at sea level, is the country's lowest point. The highest point in the country is Mount Moldoveanu. It stands about 8,347 feet (2,544 meters) high.

Left: The Black Sea is a favorite summer vacation spot for many Romanians. These people enjoy a visit to the beach in Dobruja, a region in the southeastern part of Romania.

Mount Moldoveanu is located in the Transylvanian Alps, which form part of the Carpathian Mountain Range. Hills, **plateaus**, and plains make up a large part of Romania's land. They are dotted with over 2,300 lakes. Lake Razelm, the country's largest lake, covers 160 square miles (415 sq km). Romania's largest river, the Danube River, flows along Romania's southern border for about 668 miles (1,075 km) before emptying into the Black Sea.

Above:
This man is rowing his boat through the calm waters of the Danube Delta, which is the region where the Danube River empties into the Black Sea.

Left: Children in Romania make the most of winter snow in the mountains. In February 2003, temperatures in some mountain regions dipped to an unusually cold -4° F (-20° C).

Climate

Romania has four different seasons. Summers are mostly sunny with many rain showers and some thunderstorms. Winters are cloudy, cold, and snowy. In Bucharest, Romania's capital city, temperatures can reach 86° Fahrenheit (30° Celsius) in summer and drop to 19° F (-7° C) in winter. The rainiest months are from April to June and from September to October. Romania gets an average of 25 inches (635 millimeters) of rain each year. Twice as much rain falls in the mountains as on the plains.

Plants and Animals

Forests cover about 25 percent of the country's land, including Romania's mountain regions, where trees such as beech, oak, pine, and spruce grow.

Animals such as red deer, brown bears, and lynx live in Romania. Rare antelopes called chamois live in high regions of the Carpathian Mountains. The Black Sea and the country's many rivers and lakes are also rich in animal life, including salmon, herring, and eels.

Below: Many types of birds live in the Danube Delta area, which is located on the northern edge of Romania's Black Sea coastline.

History

In about 2000 B.C., groups of people called the Thracians moved to what is now Romania. The Greeks moved into the region in the seventh century B.C. They called the Thracians the Getae. The Romans **conquered** the region, which they called Dacia, in A.D. 106. They ruled Dacia until A.D. 271. Over the next eight hundred years, several groups conquered Dacia. One of these groups, the Slavs, settled in the region. Over the years, the Slavs and Dacians combined into one **ethnic** group. They were the early **ancestors** of Romanians.

Below:
Under Roman rule, many government officials, soldiers, and traders came to Dacia. They changed Dacia's government and brought a new language, Latin. They also built many new cities.

From Hungarians to Ottoman Turks

By the early eleventh century A.D., the Hungarians had invaded. They claimed parts of Transylvania. To escape them, many Dacians moved south or east. By 1359, the Dacians had formed two separate **principalities** called Walachia and Moldavia. In the 1400s, invading Ottoman Turks took over but allowed the principalities to rule themselves. In the 1700s, the Turks took total control. The Turks often ruled dishonestly and harshly, causing many people to suffer.

Russian Rule and Independence

During the 1700s, the people of what is now Romania, especially the Orthodox Christians, often were treated very poorly. In 1774, the Russians promised to protect the Orthodox Christians. In return, the Christians supported Russia in its fight against the Ottomans. By 1829, the Russians controlled Walachia and Moldavia. The Russians later lost power. In 1859, Alexandru Cuza was elected the ruler of both Moldavia and Walachia. The two lands later joined to form one nation, Romania. In 1878, Romania gained formal independence.

Left: This drawing depicts Bucharest when it was the capital of Walachia (1659–1862). In 1862, under ruler Alexandru Cuza, Bucharest became the capital of the nation of Romania.

The Two World Wars

In 1916, Romania joined World War I and fought on the side of the Allies, which included Russia, Britain, France, and the United States. The Allies fought against Austria-Hungary and Germany. After the war, Romania gained several large pieces of land. It later lost most of those regions. In 1939, World War II began. The country fought on the side of Germany. After the Soviet Union invaded Bucharest, Romania switched sides and declared war on the Germans.

Above: The Arch of Triumph, located in Bucharest, was built to honor Romania's World War I victory over Germany and Austria-Hungary.

Left: Nicolae and Elena Ceauşescu were found guilty of causing the deaths of about sixty thousand Romanians. They had told soldiers to fire into crowds of angry citizens gathered in a city square. They were both put to death on December 25, 1989.

The Communist Years and Beyond

After World War II, Romania became a **communist** nation. It was renamed the People's Republic of Romania in 1947. In 1965, Nicolae Ceauşescu became the leader of Romania. He ruled harshly and used special police forces to take control of all political, economic, and social life in Romania. In 1989, he was taken from power after large **uprisings** broke out nationwide. Ion Iliescu was elected president in 1990. Romania has been a **democratic** nation ever since.

Stephen the Great (1435–1504)

Throughout his reign, Stephen the Great defended Romania against invasions by the Ottoman Turks, the Hungarians, and the Poles. Because he worked to defend Christianity and the Romanian people, he was called the "Athlete of Christ."

Michael the Brave (1558–1601)

Michael the Brave, prince of Walachia, conquered Transylvania and Moldavia. He was the first to unite the three lands that would become modern Romania.

King Carol I

King Carol I (1839–1914)

King Carol I was the leader who gained Romania its independence from the Ottoman Turks in the War of Independence (1877–1878).

Queen Marie

Queen Marie (1875–1938)

Famous for her charm and intelligence, Queen Marie was a great supporter of the arts. After World War I, she helped to **negotiate** Romania's gain of lands.

Government and the Economy

Romania is now a democratic **republic**. The Romanian government is made up of three main branches. The executive branch, led by the president, consists of a prime minister and the Council of Ministers. The ministers serve as advisers to the president. Parliament, or the legislative branch, is divided into the Senate and the Chamber of Deputies. The judicial branch is made up of the Supreme Court of Justice and county, local, and military courts.

Below:
This grand building is called the Palace of Parliament. It is where Romania's parliament meets. The building was known as the House of the People when the country was a communist nation.

Local Government and the Military

Romania is divided into forty-two regions. Forty-one of the regions are counties, which are called *judete* (joo-DEH-TSE). The last region, Bucharest, is a **municipality**. All of the forty-one counties and Bucharest have their own independent, local governments. Each region is led by a *prefect* (pre-FEHKT).

In Romania, all men must serve in the military. They join when they turn twenty years old. Most of them serve between twelve and eighteen months.

Above: Many tanks were brought in by Nicolae Ceaușescu to control the large antigovernment uprisings of 1989. Instead, the soldiers turned against the ruler and helped the citizens bring down Ceaușescu's government.

The Economy

The Romanian economy has struggled since the fall of communism. Money from the International Monetary Fund (IMF) allowed Romania to make steps toward a strong economy. These steps included paying money owed to other nations and **privatizing** industries. The government is also trying to control the cost of services and goods in Romania, but prices keep rising. Even with these efforts, more than 44 percent of the people in Romania lived in poverty in 2000. That number is expected to rise.

Above: Romania ships most of its **exports** to Italy, Germany, and France. Romania buys most of its goods from those same countries.

Farming and Other Industries

Wheat, corn, sugar beets, potatoes, and grapes are the main crops in Romania. Fish and caviar, or fish eggs, are other important products. Romania produces cement, machinery, and chemicals. It also produces iron, steel, and wood products. Romania used to produce oil, but it has been used up. Today, mining products include coal, iron, copper, and lead. Since the fall of communism, the tourism industry has become important.

Below: The growing of grapes and the making of wine are important industries in Romania. These vines are part of the Murfatlar vineyards in Dobruja. They are some of the best in the country.

People and Lifestyle

Romania's population is made up of many ethnic groups. The largest group is the ethnic Romanians. Others include Roma, who originally came from India, Hungarians, Ukrainians, and Germans. Small numbers of Serbs, Croats, Turks, Russians, Tatars, and other groups also live in the country. The government has officially accepted eighteen of the small ethnic groups in Romania. Each has a seat in the country's parliament.

Above: These ethnic Hungarian boys from Szek, or Sic, a village in Transylvania, are wearing traditional costumes.

Left: A girl and boy pose in a snow-covered mountain region of Romania. Women in Romania often outlive men. The women live an average of seventy-four years, while men average only sixty-seven years.

From the Countryside to the City

People in **rural** Romania have strong traditions and religious values. Their lifestyles are much different than those in **urban** areas. Many rural Romanians refuse to own modern equipment, such as washing machines and refrigerators. They prefer to use traditional methods of washing clothes and preserving food. Strict rules also control how rural men and women meet. In Romania's cities, most lifestyles are much more modern.

Above: Boys in a rural region of Romania pose with their homemade wooden carts. About 45 percent of Romanians live in rural areas. The other 55 percent live in cities, such as Bucharest, Iaşi, or Constanţa.

Family Life

Romanian families are generally very close. In the past, it was common for married children and their parents to live together. Today, many newlywed couples live in their own homes. It is still common for elderly Romanians to live with their grown children, who care for them. In Romania, having children is considered important. During the rule of Ceauşescu, married women had to have at least five children. Today, most women have just two children.

Below: Romanian newlyweds pose in traditional wedding outfits. Romanians in the cities usually get married later in life than those in the countryside.

Left: Not all children in Romania have families or homes. Many children live in orphanages or on the streets. They are sometimes called "Ceaușescu's children," because Ceaușescu was the one who ordered Romanian families to have five or more children even if the parents could not afford to raise them.

Women in Romania

In Romania, women make up about half of the **workforce**. In the cities, women usually work in the health, education, and manufacturing fields. In rural areas, most women work on farms. Romania's government has passed laws to improve working conditions for women. Women are now serving in parliament as well. Even with these changes, most women are still treated unequally and often earn less than men for doing the same job.

Education

Romanian children between ages seven and fourteen must attend school. The first four years are called elementary school. The next four years are called lower secondary school. After students complete lower secondary school, they can choose to attend secondary school. Romania has five different types of secondary schools, including general education, teacher-training, **vocational**, art, and physical education schools.

Below:
In many areas of Romania, the main language spoken is not Romanian. The students in those areas are usually taught in their own languages, which include Hungarian and German.

Higher Education

Romania has many public and private universities. These schools are often expensive. The government gives some students in public universities money to help with costs. Most study programs last for four to six years, depending on the course of study. Popular courses include medicine, law, economics, and political science. Many students enjoy taking part in programs that allow them to study in other countries for a time.

Above:
The University of Bucharest is the oldest university in Romania. It was built in 1694.

Religion

More than 80 percent of the Romanian people are Christians. There are many different groups of Christians, however, including Orthodox Christian, Catholic, and Protestant groups. About 70 percent of the people belong to the Romanian Orthodox Church. About 6 percent are Catholics who belong to either Uniate or Roman Catholic churches. Another 6 percent of Romanians are Protestant.

Other Christian groups in Romania include Presbyterians, Pentecostalists, Baptists, and Jehovah's Witnesses.

Most of the remaining 18 percent of Romanians do not belong to a religion. A small number are followers of the religion of Islam. Many Jewish people used to live in Romania, but most have moved to other countries. Some people are members of the *Căluşari* (CAH-loo-shah-ree), a religious group that dates back hundreds of years. Most of their traditions and practices are kept secret.

Above:
This **mosque** is located in the town of Constanţa. The 1991 **constitution** gave all Romanians the right to freely practice their own religious beliefs.

Left: A nun sells religious items at a shop in the Voroneţ convent, which is a house for nuns. Stephen the Great built the convent in the 1400s.

Language

The official language of Romania is Romanian. Romanian is also called Daco-Romanian. It is a Romance language, meaning it came from the Latin language. Spanish, Italian, and French are also Romance languages. Romanian is very different from those languages because Romania is located close to Hungary and to countries that speak Slavic languages. Romania now uses some Hungarian and Slavic words as well as words taken from the Turks.

Left: This building is the Romanian Academy. It was founded in 1866 and is an important center of research. More than seven million publications are housed in the academy's library.

Left: After the fall of Ceaușescu's government, many new magazines and newspapers were started in Romania. The Romanians felt they were now free to read and write about whatever they liked.

Literature

In the late 1600s, many great works of literature were published in Romania. Most of them were religious works or books of poetry.

In the 1800s, Grigore Alexandrescu became well known for his **satires** and **fables**. Mihail Eminescu is recognized for creating modern Romanian poetry. Romanian play writer Eugène Ionesco was one of the most famous authors of the twentieth century. Ionesco's works led to a new theater performance style.

Arts

Religious Architecture

Romania's religious buildings are an important part of the country's history. In Moldavia, there are many beautiful **monasteries**. Many of them were built in the 1400s and 1500s and have fancy, painted decorations on the inside and outside walls. Walachia's monasteries are known for their rich decorations. They date mostly from the 1500s and 1600s. Many buildings in Transylvania were created in the **Baroque** style.

Above: Moldavian monasteries of northern Romania are painted both inside and outside with detailed religious paintings.

Left: The Three Hierarchs Church, located in Iaşi, was built in the seventeenth century.

Above: Built in 1953, the National Opera House in Bucharest can hold about one thousand people.

Romanian Theater

Romanians love going to the theater. Some experts believe that theater in Romania dates back to the time of the Dacians. It was only after the Oravita Theater was built in 1817, however, that going to the theater became very popular. In a short time, many other theaters were built all over Romania. By the 1980s, nearly seven million Romanians were attending plays. By 1996, Romania had fifty-two theaters.

Folk Songs and Music

Singing and dancing in Romania are important in both everyday life and at major events. Romanians sing or dance during events such as weddings, funerals, and religious ceremonies. Village women sing together during and after their work. Romanians also play music on instruments, such as a violin; a *cobză* (cob-ZAH), a stringed instrument; or a *ţambal* (tsam-BAL), an instrument played like a xylophone.

Romanian Crafts

Romania is famous for its many crafts, including wooden and stone carvings, pottery, **embroidered** costumes, and handwoven carpets. Many Romanians make a living by selling crafts made at home or in village workshops. Men are usually the potters and carvers. Women usually do the sewing and weaving. The beautiful, embroidered costumes made by rural Romanian women often sell for lots of money in many other countries.

Below: Many rural Romanian women still own hand-operated looms, which they use to make colorful carpets and rugs.

Leisure

Most Romanians work very hard, but they also like to have fun. Families in Romania often take summer vacations near the Black Sea or in the Carpathian Mountains. Some people go camping, swimming, or fishing. Romanians in rural areas often house tourists on their land. Many city people enjoy staying in rural lodges to relax and enjoy nature. Romania also has many hot springs and **mineral springs**. Thousands of tourists from Romania and from other countries enjoy bathing in the springs each year.

Left: These men in Braşov are playing a game of chess. Playing chess is a popular leisure activity in Romania.

At home, many Romanians enjoy chatting over meals and spending time with family members. They also enjoy playing chess and card games, such as rummy. Only Romanians who have a lot of money can afford to pay for entertainment. They can afford to play golf or tennis, eat in restaurants, go to movies, or dance in nightclubs. Visiting museums and going to opera or theater performances are popular leisure activities. Many people also attend art festivals or cultural events.

Above: Skiing the slopes in winter and rock climbing and hiking in summer are just a few of the sports Romanians enjoy when they visit the mountains. Many Romanians also love to visit the mountains to enjoy fresh air and nature.

Soccer in Romania

Soccer is by far Romania's favorite sport. Romanians love to play soccer. They also love to watch soccer games. In 1994, the Romanian team became famous for reaching the quarterfinals of the World Cup soccer championship, which was held in the United States. Romania's soccer teams have continued to work hard. Today, many Romanian soccer players play on Italian, Spanish, English, and Dutch teams.

Below: In 1981, Romania's national soccer team played against the English team at Wembley Stadium in London.

Left: Ilie Nastase was a famous Romanian tennis player of the 1970s. He was the world's number one tennis player two years in a row, in 1972 and 1973. He went on to win more than one hundred other professional titles in his tennis career.

Other Popular Sports

Besides soccer, many Romanians also enjoy playing tennis, running, hiking, cycling, skiing, sailing, and swimming.

Many Romanian athletes have won sports competitions all over the world. In 1976, Nadia Comăneci, a Romanian gymnast, became the first person in the world to get a perfect score during the Olympics. In the 2000 Olympics, the country earned gold medals in rowing, track and field, kayaking, gymnastics, fencing, and swimming.

Festivals of the Seasons

Romanians celebrate many religious festivals and festivals that mark the four seasons. *Drăgaica* (DRAH-GUY-kah) is a festival that celebrates the summer harvest. In winter, on New Year's Eve, people celebrate *Sorcova* (SOR-KOH-vah). Children brush bunches of twigs over the heads of adults for good luck. The children usually get sweets, cakes, or money in return. One spring tradition is for a young man to give the woman he loves a red and white **amulet**.

Easter Traditions

Romania's Easter traditions are quite different from those in other countries. Romanian Easter eggs are **etched** with a *condei* (KON-day), a sharp tool that looks like a pen. Some popular patterns include flowers and crosses. Red, blue, green, and yellow are favorite colors for eggs. Easter breads are popular in Romania. They are shaped like crosses, knots, or men and often have fillings.

Below: These colorfully painted Easter eggs are a Romanian specialty.

Food

Most Romanian food is very flavorful. Preparing the food sometimes takes a long time because Romanian dishes often include many ingredients, such as meat, vegetables, herbs, and spices.

Most Romanians eat three meals a day. The main meal of the day is lunch. It usually begins with crusty bread and a bowl of sour soup. Servings of meat and potatoes or fish and salad are also eaten. Lunch often ends with dessert.

Left: In Romania, most meals begin with a small glass of *tuică* (TSOO-ee-kuh). The drink is made from plums.

Sarmale (SAR-mah-leh) is a favorite dish in Romania. It is a mixture of rice, chopped meat, onions, and spices. The mixture is wrapped in cabbage leaves and cooked in tomato sauce. Another favorite dish is *mititei* (MEE-tee-tay), or grilled sausages. Different kinds of mititei are made in different regions of the country. Most Romanians also love soup, including turkey soup made with vegetables, rice, lemon juice, parsley, and dill, a kind of herb.

Alba (county) B3–B4
Arad (county) A2–B3

Bacău (county) C2–D3
Bihor (county) A2–B3
Black Sea D5–E3
Botoşani (county)
    C2–D2
Brăila (county) D3–D4
Braşov C3
Braşov (county) C3
Bulgaria B4–E5
Bucharest C4–D4
Buzău (county) C3–D4

Călăraşi (county) D4
Caraş-Şeverin
    (county) A3–B4
Cluj (county) B2–B3
Constanţa E4
Constanţa (county)
    D4–E5
Covasna (county)
    C3–D3

Danube (river) A3–E4
Danube Delta E3–E4
Dimbovita (county)
    C3–C4
Dobruja D3–E4
Dolj (county) B4–C5

Eastern Carpathians
    C2–C3

Galaţi (county) D3
Giurgiu (county)
    C5–D4
Gorj (county) B3–B4

Harghita (county)
    C2–D3
Hunedoara (county)
    B3
Hungary A1–A3

Ialomita (county) D4
Iaşi D2
Iaşi (county) D2
Ilfov (county) C4–D4

Lake Razelm E4

Above: These children are dressed in traditional Romanian costumes.

Marmureş (county)
    B2–C2
Mehedinti (county)
    B4
Moldavia D1–D3
Moldova D1–E3
Mount
    Moldoveanu C3
Mureş (county) B3–C2

Neamţ (county) C2–D2

Olt (county) B4–C5

Prahova (county)
    C3–D4

Satu Mare (county)
    B2
Serbia and
    Montenegro
    A3–B5
Sibiu (county) B3–C3

Southern
    Carpathians
    B3–C3
Suceava (county)
    C2–D2
Szek B2

Teleorman (county)
    C4–C5
Timiş (county) A3–B3
Transylvania B3–C3
Transylvanian Alps
    B3–C3
Tulcea (county) D3–E4

Ukraine B1–E3

Vaslui (county) D2–D3
Vrancea (county) D3

Walachia B4–D4
Western Carpathians
    B2–B3

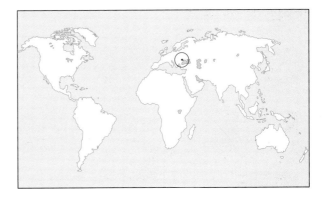

Quick Facts

Official name	Romania
Capital	Bucharest
Official Language	Romanian
Population	22,271,839 (July 2003 estimate)
Land Area	91,675 square miles (237,500 sq km)
Counties	Alba, Arad, Argeş, Bacău, Bihor, Bistriţa-Năsaud, Botoşani, Brăila, Braşov, Bucharest (municipality), Buzău, Călăraşi, Caraş-Severin, Cluj, Constanţa, Covasna, Dîmboviţa, Dolj, Galaţi, Giurgiu, Gorj, Harghita, Hunedoara, Ialomita, Iaşi, Ilfov, Maramureş, Mehedinti, Mureş, Neamţ, Olt, Prahova, Sălaj, Satu Mare, Sibiu, Suceava, Teleorman, Timiş, Tulcea, Vaslui, Vîlcea, Vrancea.
Highest Point	Mount Moldoveanu 8,347 feet (2,544 m)
Ethnic Groups	Romanians, Hungarians, Roma, Germans, Ukrainians
Main Religion	Romanian Orthodox Christianity
Major Festivals	Spring Amulet, Drăguica, Sorcova, Easter, Christmas
Currency	Leu (32,251 Romanian Leu = U.S. $1 as of 2004)

Opposite: This beautiful building is the Putna Monastery in Suceava County.

Glossary

amulet: a small charm that is believed to bring good luck or protect against evil.

ancestors: family members from the past, farther back than grandparents.

Baroque: a style of the 1600s and 1700s that used fancy, flowery designs.

communist: related to a government that owns all property in the country.

conquered: invaded and took over.

constitution: a set of laws for a country that tells what rights citizens have.

democratic: relating to a government in which citizens can elect their leaders.

embroidered: decorated a piece of cloth or clothes with fancy sewing.

etched: scratched a design into the surface of an object.

ethnic: related to a race or a culture that has similar customs and languages.

exports (n): products sent out of a country to be sold in another country.

fables: fiction stories that teach lessons.

invasions: acts of groups who enter a region to take land or valuables.

mineral springs: springs that are soaked with chemicals from the ground.

monasteries: houses for religious people, such as monks or priests.

mosque: a house of worship for those who follow the Islamic religion.

municipality: a big city area that has some power to govern itself.

negotiate: to talk to others to decide on a deal or to make a decision.

plateaus: wide, flat areas of land that are surrounded by lower land.

principalities: lands ruled by princes.

privatizing: changing from government ownership of industries to ownership by private businesses or individuals.

republic: a country in which citizens elect their own lawmakers.

rural: related to the countryside.

satires: stories that make fun of a particular problem or subject.

uprisings: acts of violence by citizens to fight against a government's rules.

urban: related to cities and large towns.

vocational: related to an occupation, profession, or skilled trade.

workforce: the people in a country who work, most often outside the home.

More Books to Read

Danube: Cyanide Spill. Environmental Disasters series. Nichol Bryan (World Almanac)

Genovieva: A True Story from Romania. Samuel Grandjean (Eastern European Aid Association)

The Gift of a Traveler. Wendy Matthews (Troll Communications)

Gypsies. Endangered Cultures series. Elizabeth Sirimarco (Smart Apple Media)

The Impudent Rooster: A Romanian Folktale. Sabina I. Rascol (Dutton Books)

Miracle of Tears. Maira von Romania (Bluestar Communications Corp.)

Romanian Folk Art: A Guide to Living Traditions. Karsten D. McNulty (Aid to Artisans)

Solid Gold: Gymnastics Stars. Darice Bailer (Random House)

Videos

A 100 Years of Lies—the Romanian Castle of Bran known as Dracula's Castle (George Angelescu)

Ceausescu: The Unrepentant Tyrant Host. Biography International series (A & E Home Video)

Germany and Romania. Great Castles of Europe series (Discovery Communication)

The Impaler—Vlad Dracula, also known as Vlad The Impaler (George Angelescu)

Web Sites

academickids.com/world/geos/ro.html

ici.ro/romania/

romaniatourism.com/album.html

visiteurope.com/Romania/

Due to the dynamic nature of the Internet, some web sites stay current longer than others. To find additional web sites, use a reliable search engine with one or more of the following keywords to help you locate information about Romania. Keywords: *Bucharest, Carpathian Mountains, Nicolae Ceauşescu, Danube, Mount Moldoveanu.*

Index